ARTIFICIAL INTELLIGENCE ETHICS AND DEBATES

Tracy Abell

www.focusreaders.com

Focus Readers is distributed by North Star Editions:
sales@northstareditions.com | 888-417-0195

Produced for Focus Readers by Red Line Editorial.

Content Consultant: Magy Seif El-Nasr, Associate Professor of Khoury College of Computer Sciences, Northeastern University

Photographs ©: Sergey Mamontov/Sputnik/AP Images, cover, 1; Shan he/Imaginechina/AP Images, 4–5; IGphotography/iStockphoto, 7; ChaNaWiT/Shutterstock Images, 8–9; Wove Love/Shutterstock Images, 11; Zapp2Photo/Shutterstock Images, 12; BigTunaOnline/Shutterstock Images, 14–15; Jeramey Lende/Shutterstock Images, 17; Red Line Editorial, 18, 39; Matej Kastelic/Shutterstock Images, 20–21; Bryan Woolston/Reuters/Newscom, 23; Damian Dovarganes/AP Images, 25; Rachel Murray/Stringer/Getty Images Entertainment/Getty Images, 27; Jenson/Shutterstock Images, 28–29; SolStock/iStockphoto, 31; Monkey Business Images/Shutterstock Images, 33; Paul Crock/AFP/Getty Images, 34–35; Gorodenkoff/Shutterstock Images, 37; Mario Suriani/AP Images, 40–41; puhhha/Shutterstock Images, 43; Ikars/Shutterstock Images, 45

Library of Congress Cataloging-in-Publication Data
Names: Abell, Tracy, author.
Title: Artificial intelligence ethics and debates / by Tracy Abell.
Description: Lake Elmo, MN : Focus Readers, 2020. | Series: Artificial
   intelligence | Includes index. | Audience: Grades 7 to 8.
Identifiers: LCCN 2019027291 (print) | LCCN 2019027292 (ebook) | ISBN
   9781644930731 (hardcover) | ISBN 9781644931523 (paperback) | ISBN
   9781644933107 (pdf) | ISBN 9781644932315 (ebook)
Subjects: LCSH: Artificial intelligence--Moral and ethical
   aspects--Juvenile literature.
Classification: LCC Q335.4 .A24 2020 (print) | LCC Q335.4 (ebook) | DDC
   170--dc23
LC record available at https://lccn.loc.gov/2019027291
LC ebook record available at https://lccn.loc.gov/2019027292

Printed in the United States of America
Mankato, MN
012020

ABOUT THE AUTHOR

Tracy Abell lives in the Rocky Mountain foothills where she enjoys running on the trails. When she's not trail running, Tracy enjoys learning new things. She's researched and written books about compost tumblers, 3D printing, drones, vending machines, and toilets. She has notebooks filled with ideas for other books.

TABLE OF CONTENTS

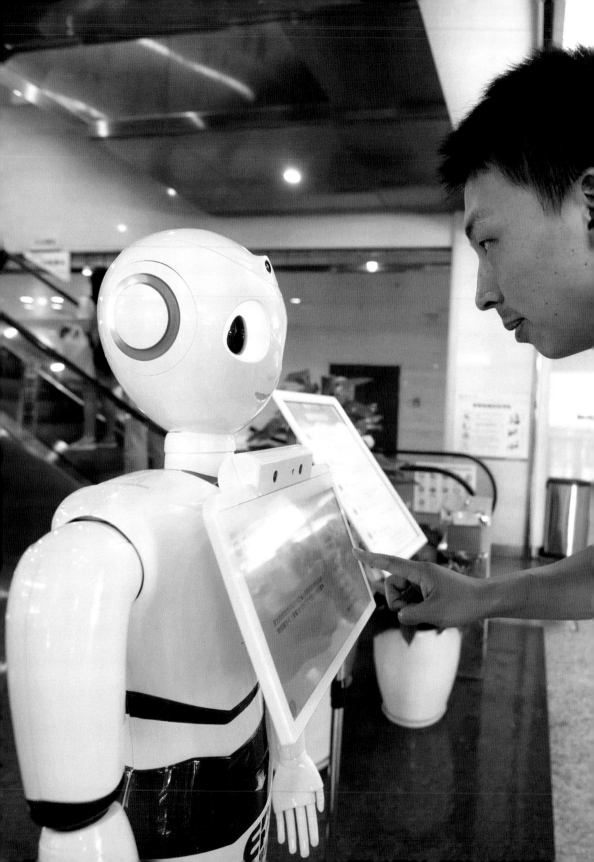

CHAPTER 1

ARTIFICIAL INTELLIGENCE

In 2017, a robot named Xiaoyi passed the exam to be a doctor in China. Xiaoyi was the first artificial intelligence (AI) to pass the test. Not only did it pass, but it also scored 96 points higher than the required score. A year later, another AI took the test to be a doctor in the United Kingdom. It scored higher than any human.

AI is the study and engineering of intelligent machines. Driverless cars are an example of AI.

A visitor to a Chinese hospital interacts with Xiaoyi in 2018.

Virtual assistant Siri is another example. **Machine learning** is also a subset of AI.

To begin the process of machine learning, people feed computer programs large amounts of data. In some cases, people have already categorized the data. AI programs then train on this data. They learn to apply those categories to new data. They make predictions about new data based on what they learned from the old data.

In other cases, people have not labeled the data. AI programs analyze the data without human input. They find new patterns in the data. Machine learning is how social media sites know which content will appeal to each user. It is also how online sellers know which products people might want to buy.

As in the case of medical exams, AI can sometimes outperform humans. But scoring

▲ Driverless cars can sense their environments and move without human input.

better than doctors on a test isn't the same as being a better doctor. Many AI experts are excited for how AI might improve human lives. But many of those same experts are concerned about granting decision-making power to AI.

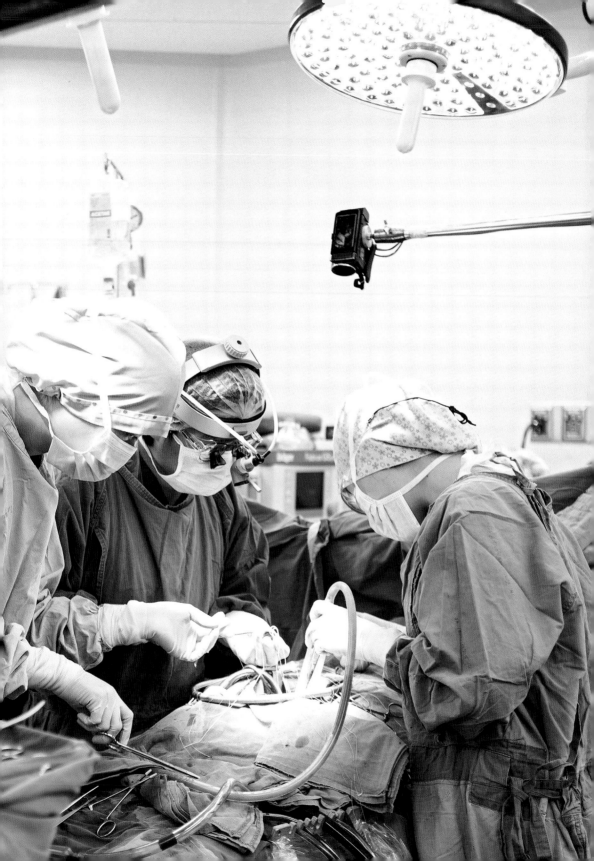

CHAPTER 2

AI IN HEALTH CARE

machine learning works well only if the data is good. Incomplete or **biased** data can cause an AI program to make wrong conclusions. This problem leads some people to question AI's value in settings such as hospitals. Machine learning already plays a role in modern health care. But people are still debating how much responsibility AI should be given.

In a hospital setting, a wrong conclusion could lead to a patient's death.

AI can help doctors and nurses do their jobs. For instance, AI's focus on patterns can help with patient records. AI software can go through patients' medical files much faster than doctors can. AI can also summarize the information. It can help doctors understand their patients' conditions.

AI can also help doctors with triage. In this process, doctors decide which patients to see first. The order is based on the urgency of each patient's medical problems. AI can help determine this order. For example, AI can read chest X-rays. It looks at the scans. It tells doctors which patients need care right away.

Experts also hope AI can help with diagnosis. The company IBM designed a powerful computer program called Watson to help cancer patients. IBM trained Watson on data from previous cancer

Hospitals are often packed with people seeking medical attention. Doctors must quickly decide who to see first.

cases. Watson learned to suggest treatments for new patients.

But Watson made mistakes. The program suggested unsafe and incorrect treatments for some patients. Fortunately, no patients were hurt. Doctors reviewed Watson's recommendations and realized they were wrong. Watson had been trained on made-up cases instead of real-life cancer cases. The AI program didn't know as much as the doctors. It had been given poor data.

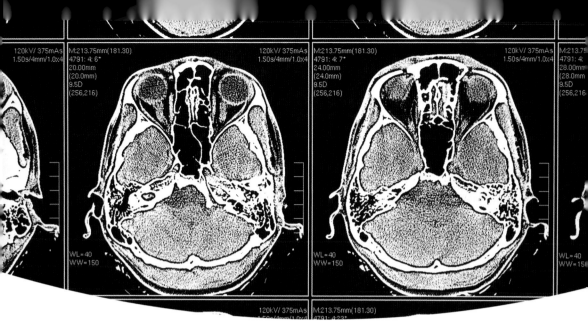

▲ AI programs can be trained to look at brain scans for signs of cancer.

Problems can also occur when AI is asked to interpret data. For example, small changes in medical notes can cause big differences in an AI program's interpretation of them. Doctors might use terms that the AI program interprets in different ways. The term "alcohol abuse" could result in a different AI summary and treatment plan than "alcohol dependence."

Another concern is that machine-learning **apps** often run as **black boxes**. Doctors have no way of knowing how a program made its decisions. They have to decide whether to accept the AI program's conclusions.

Many doctors do not yet trust AI to make good decisions. Patients also have concerns about AI in health care. In a 2018 survey, 25 percent of respondents said they would not use AI health care services. Some doctors and hospitals are taking a careful approach with AI. They only use it for lower-risk work such as record keeping. That way the AI program gains more knowledge about medical issues. Only later will they consider using AI in higher-risk processes.

THINK ABOUT IT ◄

What are the advantages and disadvantages of involving AI in making diagnoses? Would you want AI making a medical diagnosis for you? Why or why not?

CHAPTER 3

DATA AND PRIVACY

Artificial intelligence can make studying health care data easier. It also makes handling large amounts of data easier in general. But there is a cost for the people whose data is being collected. For example, people often encounter AI without realizing it. As a result, they don't know when they are sharing data. People may not know what data is being collected about them. And they may not know what that data is being used for.

Apps on smartphones collect data about their users.

Sites such as Google and Facebook collect data from users. People use the site for free in exchange for their data. Every action a user takes on the site gives more data to the AI program running it. Through **data mining**, the AI program learns more about the user's likes and interests. Sites sell that data to other companies. Those companies then target the user with ads.

Many users believe ads are a fair trade for using the sites for free. Data mining also gives them a customized experience online. They see content chosen for them based on their interests. However, other users worry about privacy.

> ## ➤ THINK ABOUT IT

Do you think data collection is a fair trade for the free use of websites? What personal information would you be concerned about companies having access to?

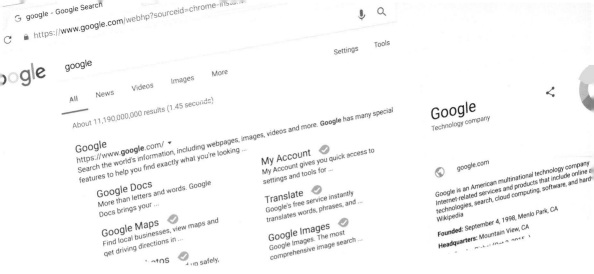

The AI program running Google collects information about users' search history.

Many people view privacy as a matter of informed consent. They choose what information to share and how it will be used. But online data can be collected and reused in many ways. People don't always have control over what happens to their personal data.

For example, data brokers buy personal data from the companies people do business with. The brokers then package the data in different ways. They may categorize it by age, gender, education, or interests. Then they sell the data.

One data broker sold lists of senior citizens. Companies targeted that list of people. They convinced many senior citizens to buy things they didn't need.

Aside from online sites, cell phones are another huge source of data. Cell phones constantly

HOW DATA BROKERS WORK

Data brokers get people's information from a variety of online and offline sources. They take that information and create lists of people based on certain categories. Data brokers sell these lists to companies, which can then target their ads to specific groups of people.

Sources of Data	Types of Data Collected	Sample Categories/Lists
social media profiles	full name	sports enthusiasts
purchase history	address	music lovers
free-to-play games or apps	email address	impulsive buyers
government records	telephone number	people with mental health issues
search history	age and birth date	people who recently got married
	gender	expectant parents
	Social Security number	
	income	
	education	
	occupation	
	race or ethnicity	
	sexual orientation	
	marital status	
	interests	

collect data. For instance, they keep track of calls made and received. They track text messages. A cell phone also constantly updates its location. The phone company needs that information to figure out which cell tower is closest. But phone companies also sell that data. As a result, nearby stores can send ads to the phone.

AI has also made government **surveillance** easier. Before AI, governments collected data on only a few people. That data took lots of time and money to analyze. But with AI, many governments collect data from as many people as possible.

In 2017, the US National Security Agency (NSA) obtained more than 534 million records of phone calls and text messages. That's more than three times what the NSA gathered in 2016. All that data makes it easier for the government to target certain groups of people, often unfairly.

CHAPTER 4

BIASES IN AI

People have given artificial intelligence a lot of power. For example, some organizations use AI to streamline their processes. AI helps people make decisions in hiring, prison sentencing, and policing. But biases in AI **algorithms** can result in unfair decisions.

Critics point out the lack of diversity in the field of AI. Fewer than 2 percent of people doing technical jobs for Facebook and Google are black.

White men make up the vast majority of people working in AI.

Women hold only 20 percent of the technical jobs at eight large tech companies. The people creating AI systems are mostly white men. Studies show AI programs have the same biases as the people who programmed them.

AI biases can directly impact people's lives. For example, Amazon used AI in its hiring process. The program could read through job applications quickly. But Amazon eventually discovered that it had a bias against applications from women.

Biases also cause problems in the justice system. AI programs assess how likely it is that offenders will commit crimes in the future. Judges use these risk assessments to decide who can be set free and who should spend time in prison. However, studies have found that the AI programs can be unreliable. For example, black people are more likely to be given high-risk scores but not

▲ The amount of time many offenders spend in prison is partly determined by AI.

actually re-offend. Meanwhile, white people are more likely to be given low-risk scores yet go on to commit other crimes.

Some police departments use AI for **predictive policing**. The goal is to predict where crimes might happen. Then police officers can patrol those areas to prevent crimes. But biased data results in biased predictions. For example, the AI program uses arrest data to make its predictions.

White people break drug laws at equal rates as people of color. Yet drug arrests are much higher for black and Latino people than for white people. The program predicts problems in black and Latino neighborhoods. Police patrols go there. They make more arrests. As a result, predictive policing can lead to a cycle of injustice.

Joy Buolamwini is a black computer scientist. She studied gender and racial bias in AI systems. In one study, she showed AI programs many different faces. The programs recognized most light-skinned male faces. They were wrong only 1 percent of the time. But those same programs had trouble with dark-skinned female faces. They identified the women as male 35 percent of the time. They were even wrong about famous people such as Michelle Obama and Oprah Winfrey. As a result of her research, Buolamwini started the

△ An AI program sifts through a variety of data and creates reports that guide police to patrol certain parts of a city.

Algorithmic Justice League. The organization raises awareness of bias in algorithms. It provides a place to report software biases.

AI4ALL

Fei-Fei Li is a professor of computer science at Stanford University. She believes AI programs are likely to have built-in biases if only men or white people create them. She wants to increase diversity in AI. To do this, she cofounded the organization AI4ALL.

The goal of AI4ALL is to get more young people interested in AI careers. AI4ALL especially wants more people from underrepresented groups to work in AI. These groups include students from lower-income backgrounds. They include women and people of color. AI4ALL also wants non-binary and LGBTQ students to work in AI.

AI4ALL offers summer programs at various US colleges. The sessions offer problem-solving and hands-on learning. They also provide mentor opportunities with people working in AI. By attending the programs, students become part

⚓ Fei-Fei Li speaks about diversity in tech companies at the 2018 MAKERS Conference in Los Angeles.

of a lifelong network. It is called Changemakers in AI. This network provides access to continuing education and internship support. It also helps students with college preparation.

Many of the programs are free or low-cost. Financial aid is available. AI4ALL also offers Open Learning. This is a free program for high school students. It can be used online or as an in-person team project. Students gain AI technical skills. They build their own AI projects. They also debate the social and ethical impacts of AI.

CHAPTER 5

AI IN THE WORKFORCE

Artificial intelligence can do some work more efficiently than humans. For example, AI can analyze data 100 times more quickly than humans. It can save workers time and effort. But AI is also changing the job market. Some people are concerned AI might replace human workers in some fields entirely. The human workers will be left jobless. Other people say AI will create new jobs for humans.

Many jobs that used to require human workers are now done by robots.

A study released in 2019 predicted 25 percent of US jobs could be lost to AI. Some jobs might disappear in the next few years. Others might not disappear for another 20 years. Women and people of color are at the highest risk of losing their jobs to AI. Women hold the majority of office positions. Those jobs are easily **automated**. Cashier positions are also vulnerable. Experts expect that 97 percent of cashiers will lose their jobs to AI in the coming years. In 2016, 73 percent of cashiers were women.

Not all jobs are at risk from AI. Experts say there will still be plenty of work requiring human intelligence. For example, workers with social and emotional skills will be in high demand. These jobs include doctors, nurses, and social workers. The field of health care will further expand because of a worldwide aging population.

▲ Many stores now have self-service kiosks. Customers can pay without interacting with a human cashier.

Also, humans are still better than AI at creativity. People can expect job growth in industries requiring creative thinking. Experts also predict increased demand for engineers, teachers, managers, and computer specialists.

The jobs are there. But people need the right training and education to access them. Experts predict millions of people will need to change jobs by 2030. Additionally, many workers will need to move to completely different industries. People will need to learn new skills. This will be hard for older workers. And not everyone will have equal access to retraining. Experts identify a need for programs and resources to help people transition to new jobs.

People have various ideas about how to help with job loss. One idea is to have the government pay everyone $1,000 per month. That money would offset the jobs lost to AI. Another idea is connected to machine learning. People would receive a small payment each time they share personal data. For example, giving data to a social media site helps the site create better algorithms.

Experts predict an increase in jobs in health care. But those jobs require specialized training and skills.

Better algorithms result in more users on the site. That person's data helps the business grow. People could share in the business's profits by getting paid for their valuable data.

CHAPTER 6

AI IN THE MILITARY

Artificial intelligence is changing more than just the job market. It is also affecting the military. Some people believe military AI will save lives. But others believe it will result in more wars.

Militaries use AI in pilot training. For example, pilots develop their skills in virtual programs. The AI programs create unpredictable events. The pilots must adapt to the new situations. This training could save their lives in combat.

Fighter pilots can train on flight simulators without being in real danger.

Military doctors also benefit from AI. They train on robots programmed with a variety of medical conditions. They can apply this training to real combat. They learn how to save human soldiers' lives.

Militaries also use AI in surveillance. Drones take pictures and videos of enemy areas. AI analyzes that data. It can help militaries find missing soldiers. It can help distinguish between enemy soldiers and **civilians**. Ultimately, it can help militaries identify threats without human soldiers having to enter dangerous areas.

Not everyone agrees that AI should be involved in war. For example, Google sold AI algorithms to the US military. These algorithms helped improve the military's ability to target drone strikes. Several Google employees quit in protest. Thousands more signed a petition

Soldiers can send military drones into enemy areas for surveillance.

saying they didn't want their work used in warfare. Google leadership listened to its employees. The company did not renew the military contract.

Some people worry about AI gaining more power. As of 2019, humans controlled all military drones. But the US Army is developing a new drone that would be able to target people on its own. It would decide who to kill with little human input. Many people worry about this development.

CAMPAIGN TO STOP KILLER ROBOTS

The Campaign to Stop Killer Robots is made up of more than 100 organizations. They come from 54 countries. The campaign wants a ban on **autonomous weapons**. Members believe humans should have control over the use of military force. They argue that AI cannot make ethical decisions about who should live or die.

According to the campaign, having AI weapons would make it easier for countries to go to war. When human soldiers fight, people worry about injury and death. In contrast, countries might not be concerned about sending robots into battle. The group also worries that so-called killer robots might be used on civilians. For instance, governments could use them in police work or to stop protests.

AUTONOMOUS WEAPONS: SUPPORT AND OPPOSITION

Support the Ban		Oppose the Ban
Algeria	Ghana	Australia
Argentina	Guatemala	Belgium
Austria	Iraq	France
Bolivia	Mexico	Germany
Brazil	Morocco	Israel
Chile	Nicaragua	Russia
China*	Pakistan	South Korea
Colombia	Palestine	Spain
Costa Rica	Panama	Sweden
Cuba	Peru	Turkey
Djibouti	Uganda	United Kingdom
Ecuador	Vatican City	United States
Egypt	Venezuela	
El Salvador	Zimbabwe	

*China specified that it wanted to ban the use of the weapons, but not their development or production.

As of November 2018, 28 countries supported a ban on fully autonomous weapons.

Other people believe autonomous weapons could save human lives. Human soldiers wouldn't need to enter direct combat as often. Robots would fight instead. People also argue that AI might make better judgments than human soldiers. AI does not experience stress or fear. It does not get tired. It can process situations more quickly than human soldiers can.

CHAPTER 7

AI RIGHTS AND THE FUTURE

In 1942, author Isaac Asimov wrote a short story that presented three rules for robots. The first rule said robots must not harm humans or let humans be harmed. The second rule said robots must follow humans' orders. The only exception is if those orders go against the first rule. The third rule said robots should protect themselves. Again, the only exception is if that self-protection goes against the first two rules.

Isaac Asimov anticipated some of the questions people have today about AI.

AI is advancing at a fast rate. Most experts agree that Asimov's three rules are not enough anymore. Some people suggest designing friendly AI. Friendly AI means programs that want to follow the rules. This is different from forcing AI to follow rules. For example, one researcher believes AI programs should be designed to follow an ethical direction. He thinks machine learning could gain ethical knowledge and grow the way humans do.

Other people suggest clarifying Asimov's first law. It could include the idea of human rights. Court systems already recognize these rights. Any time an AI system took away a person's rights, it would be considered harm.

AI raises questions about legal responsibility. Many people work on an AI system. If a system causes harm, a judge or jury will need to decide

▲ It is unclear who is responsible for an AI program: the company that built it, the programmer, or the program.

who to hold responsible. If humans are held responsible, there's an assumption that the system is under human control. But not everyone agrees that AI should be under human control.

One technology writer is concerned about AI civil rights. He disagrees with Asimov's rules. He believes it would be wrong to program AI to never harm humans. He thinks that would be like putting an animal in a cage. He believes humans have a moral duty to never control AI that way.

Other people believe robots will get smarter and act more like humans. They want laws to protect robots. They want rights for automated workers. In 2018, the European Union (EU) considered a proposal to give human rights to autonomous robots. Many AI experts thought that was a bad idea. They said the proposal was based on incorrect ideas of what AI robots are

➤ THINK ABOUT IT

What rules, if any, do you think AI should follow?

▲ The European Union is a political and economic organization of European countries.

capable of. They believed it would be wrong to give legal status to AI. The EU dropped the plan.

Many people fear that technology will reach the Singularity. This term refers to a future point at which machines become smarter than humans. At this point, AI would be outside of human control. AI might decide it doesn't need people anymore. Whether or not the Singularity occurs, AI will continue to present debates and ethical considerations. It will be up to humans to decide the role AI will play in society.

ARTIFICIAL INTELLIGENCE ETHICS AND DEBATES

Write your answers on a separate piece of paper.

1. Write a paragraph summarizing one of the debates around artificial intelligence.

2. Do you believe it's a good idea for cell phone companies to sell personal data? Why or why not?

3. What is the name for an app that operates with no way of telling how it makes its decisions?

    A. an algorithm
    B. a bias
    C. a black box

4. What might happen if an AI program recommended an unusual medical treatment?

    A. The doctor would accept and follow the recommendation without question.
    B. The doctor would use a different AI to find out what it recommends for treatment.
    C. The doctor would review the patient's medical records and come up with a new treatment plan.

Answer key on page 48.

GLOSSARY

algorithms
Steps that a computer must follow to complete a process.

apps
Computer programs that complete a task.

automated
Operated by machines with minimal human input.

autonomous weapons
Weapons that can launch strikes on their own, without human involvement.

biased
Unfairly prejudiced for or against a person or group of people.

black boxes
The unknown internal workings of computer systems.

civilians
People who are not in the military.

data mining
Collecting and analyzing huge amounts of data to find patterns and predict trends.

machine learning
A subset of AI in which a computer analyzes data to find patterns and make decisions on its own.

predictive policing
The use of data systems to predict and prevent crime.

surveillance
Close observation or monitoring.

TO LEARN MORE

BOOKS

Hulick, Kathryn. *Artificial Intelligence*. Minneapolis: Abdo Publishing, 2016.

Jackson, Tom. *Will Robots Ever Be Smarter Than Humans? Theories About Artificial Intelligence*. New York: Gareth Stevens Publishing, 2019.

McPherson, Stephanie Sammartino. *Artificial Intelligence: Building Smarter Machines*. Minneapolis: Twenty-First Century Books, 2018.

NOTE TO EDUCATORS

Visit **www.focusreaders.com** to find lesson plans, activities, links, and other resources related to this title.

INDEX

Answer Key: 1. Answers will vary; 2. Answers will vary; 3. C; 4. C